**Dear Parents,**

Welcome to the Scholastic Reader series. We have taken over 80 years of experience with teachers, parents, and children and put it into a program that is designed to match your child's interests and skills.

**Level 1**—Short sentences and stories made up of words kids can sound out using their phonics skills and words that are important to remember.

**Level 2**—Longer sentences and stories with words kids need to know and new "big" words that they will want to know.

**Level 3**—From sentences to paragraphs to longer stories, these books have large "chunks" of texts and are made up of a rich vocabulary.

**Level 4**—First chapter books with more words and fewer pictures.

It is important that children learn to read well enough to succeed in school and beyond. Here are ideas for reading this book with your child:

- Look at the book together. Encourage your child to read the title and make a prediction about the story.
- Read the book together. Encourage your child to sound out words when appropriate. When your child struggles, you can help by providing the word.
- Encourage your child to retell the story. This is a great way to check for comprehension.
- Have your child take the fluency test on the last page to check progress.

Scholastic Readers are designed to support your child's efforts to learn how to read at every age and every stage. Enjoy helping your child learn to read and love to read.

**—Francie Alexander**
    Chief Education Officer
    Scholastic Education

*For Irene O'Garden and Walt Whitman*
*—J. Marzollo*

*For my niece Emma, with love*
*—J. Moffatt*

Text copyright © 1996 by Jean Marzollo.
Illustrations copyright © 1996 by Judith Moffatt.
Activities copyright © 2003 Scholastic Inc.

Library of Congress Cataloging-in-Publication Data is available.

ISBN 0-590-26587-3

10 9                                                                     06 07

Printed in the U.S.A.     23
First printing, July 1996

# I Am Water

by Jean Marzollo
Illustrated by Judith Moffatt

## Scholastic Reader — Level 1

SCHOLASTIC INC.
New York   Toronto   London   Auckland   Sydney
Mexico City   New Delhi   Hong Kong   Buenos Aires

Watch me.
I am water.
I am home for the fish.

I am rain for the earth.

I am drink for the people.

I am bathwater for babies.

I am all that,
and I am more.

I am water for cooking.

I am ice for cooling.

# I am snow for sledding.

I am pools for splashing.

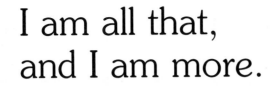

I am all that,
and I am more.

# I am puddles for boots.

I am rivers for boats.

I am lakes for swimming.

I am waves for watching.

I am all that,
and I am more.

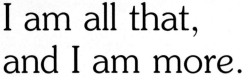

Watch me.
Watch over me.
I am water.